MUS
SET
D1147980
DISCARDED
Northamptonshire Libraries

HOLY BOY

A FOLK ORATORIO

with words and music by
DAVID PALMER

'Holy Boy' begins with the story of David, the shepherd boy who became king, and follows the plight of the Jewish nation throughout the years of the Old Testament – mentioning in particular the prophecies of Isaiah, and the coming of a Messiah – Emmanuel. It continues into the New Testament with the story of the birth of Christ from the Annunciation to the Flight into Egypt.

The work is suitable for either small or large groups of performers, with the backing of any instrumental combination (e.g. guitars, recorders, piano or orchestra), and there are a number of opportunities for solo singers.

In this edition, 'Holy Boy' is arranged for a two part choir (with occasional three or four part optional 'extras'), soloists and an accompaniment of piano and/or guitar with suggestions for recorders and melodic percussion instruments.

It is recommended that an audience rehearsal of 15 to 20 minutes precedes the performance. Part I (up to No.14) could then be followed by an interval, and Part II would complete the performance. The total duration is approximately 75 minutes.

The suggested numbers for audience participation are:-

No.2 **'So The Bible Says'** *(same tune also for No's 10 & 20)*
No.12 **'Emmanuel'** *(also No.14)*
No.13 **'Ever Bowing, Ever Scraping'** *(split audience into two to sing the chorus)*
No.22 **'Shelter Me Friend'**
No.27 **'Holy Child'** *(which the audience sings through twice whilst the choir divides into two, then three parts during the second rendition!)*
No.31 **'Holy Boy'** *(the chorus after each verse, and the ending where the audience could try singing lines 1 & 2 in the score)*

This seems a lot, but we have found through experience that the audience will pick up these melodies very quickly. Let the choir start singing and invite the audience to join in as soon as they can.

Because of the nature of this work, it is thought that the audience should be asked not to applaud during the performance – except if they wish, at the end of each part.

Some of the songs in 'Holy Boy' are very suitable for general school or church use, for assemblies or services, or for concert performance. For Christmas, it would be quite feasible to produce just Part II of the work, or to combine songs from 'Holy Boy' with traditional carols. Whichever way you use it, I sincerely hope you will enjoy the music of 'Holy Boy'.

David J. Palmer

Orchestral parts available on hire from the publisher

Cover Design: CAROL LOGAN
ISBN 0 86175 078 0

HOLY BOY

A FOLK ORATORIO

CONTENTS

PART I

PART II

PART I

1. Shepherd, Lonely Shepherd

(Soloist)

2. So The Bible Says

(Chorus)

3. Recit: The King Of Israel

(2 Soloists)

4. Go To Bethlehem

(2 Soloists and 2 Choruses)

Ah,
Ah,
So it came to pass as the Lord had pre - scribed, one of
will be the one.
f (glock.)
Ah,
Jes - se's sons as al - rea - dy des - cribed, he was a shep-herd boy,
Ah,
just a
Ah,
Ah,
shep-herd boy,
Ah,
mf
Here in Beth-le - hem,
right here in Beth-le - hem,
Ah,
Ah,
dim.
Here in Beth-le - hem,
Poco rit.
right here in Beth-le - hem.
mp
Ah,
Ah,
Ah,
attacca

5. Recit: So David Was Anointed

(2 Soloists)

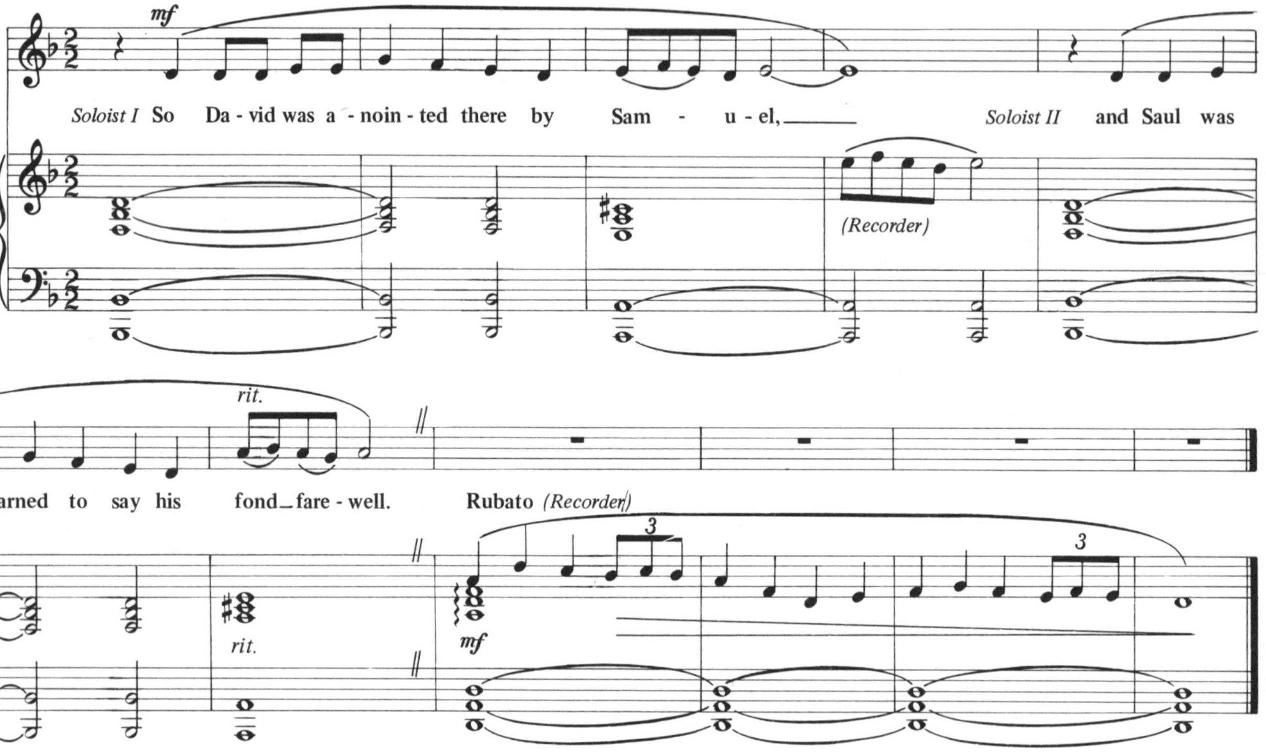

mf

Soloist I So Da - vid was a - noin - ted there by Sam - u - el, *Soloist II* and Saul was

(Recorder)

warned to say his fond fare - well.

rit.

Rubato *(Recorder)*

3

rit.

mf

3

6. Song Of The Kings (Part 1)

(2 Soloists and Chorus)

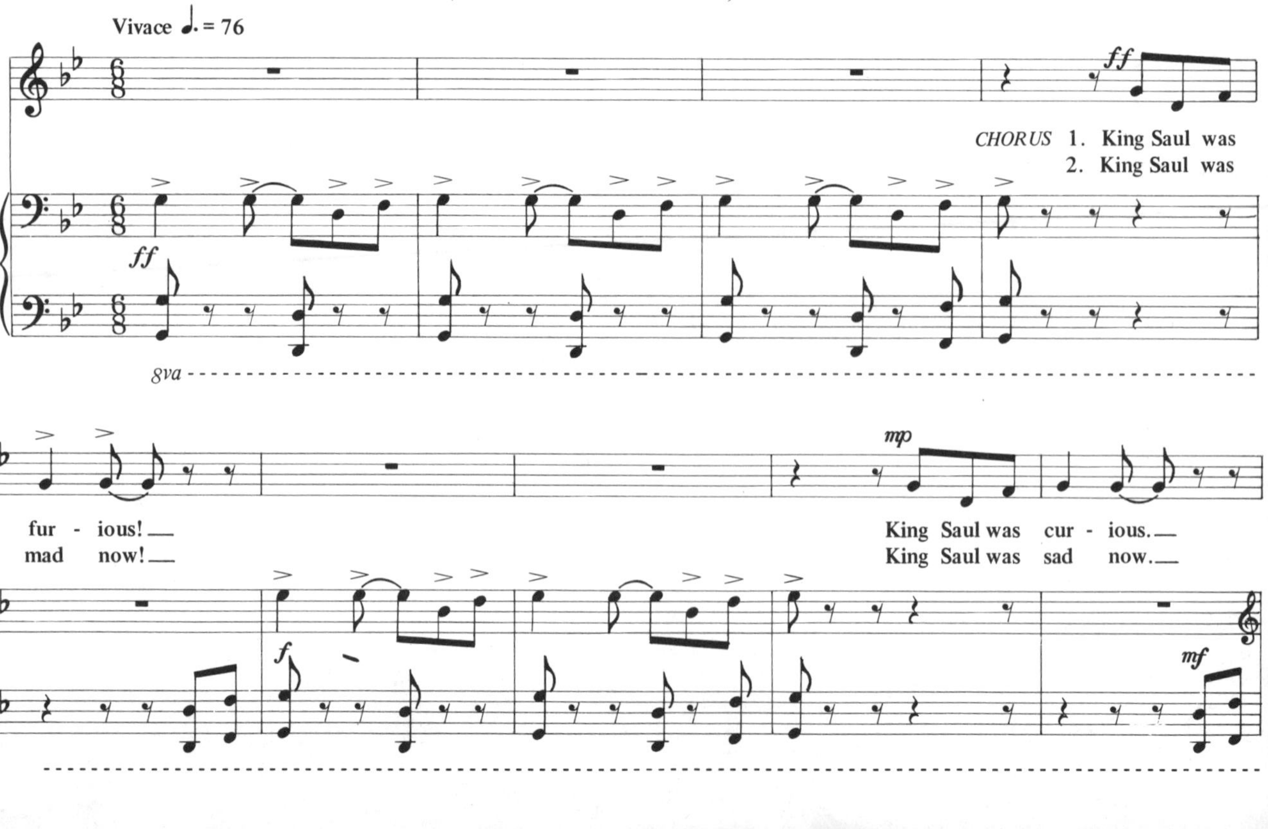

C Bb F C
mf
Soloist I Who would suc - ceed him was most on his mind.
Some - one sug - ges - ted that mu - sic would calm.
mp
C Bb F C C Fm To Coda Gb G
Soloist II Who it would be he was an - xious to find.
Soloist I The Lord had re - buked him and warned him
Soloist II of change; But
Some - one said Da - vid might have just the charm. The harp he would play to the
C Fm Gb G No Chord
ff
when would it hap - pen the feel - ing was strange.
CHORUS It was so strange!
mp
8va
D.C. al Coda
CODA Gb G No Chord
sheep as they grazed.
Soloist II When Saul heard him play he was tru - ly a - mazed!

7. The Lord Is My Shepherd

(Soloist — boy preferably — and Chorus)

F A 1,2 Am
mf
let me be your sheep.
Soloist 2. My
3. A
p
3 Am Am G
Soloist 4. His good - ness and kind - ness shall fol - low me and be
p mp
F C Dm Am
with me all my days; in his house di-vine, to the end of time
Dm E No Chord Am
I will hon-our him for ev - er more, my Lord,
CHORUS My
mp
F Dm rit. A
my Lord, my Lord, my Lord.
Lord, my Lord, my Lord, my Lord.
p
8va

8. Recit: So David Freed The King

(2 Soloists)

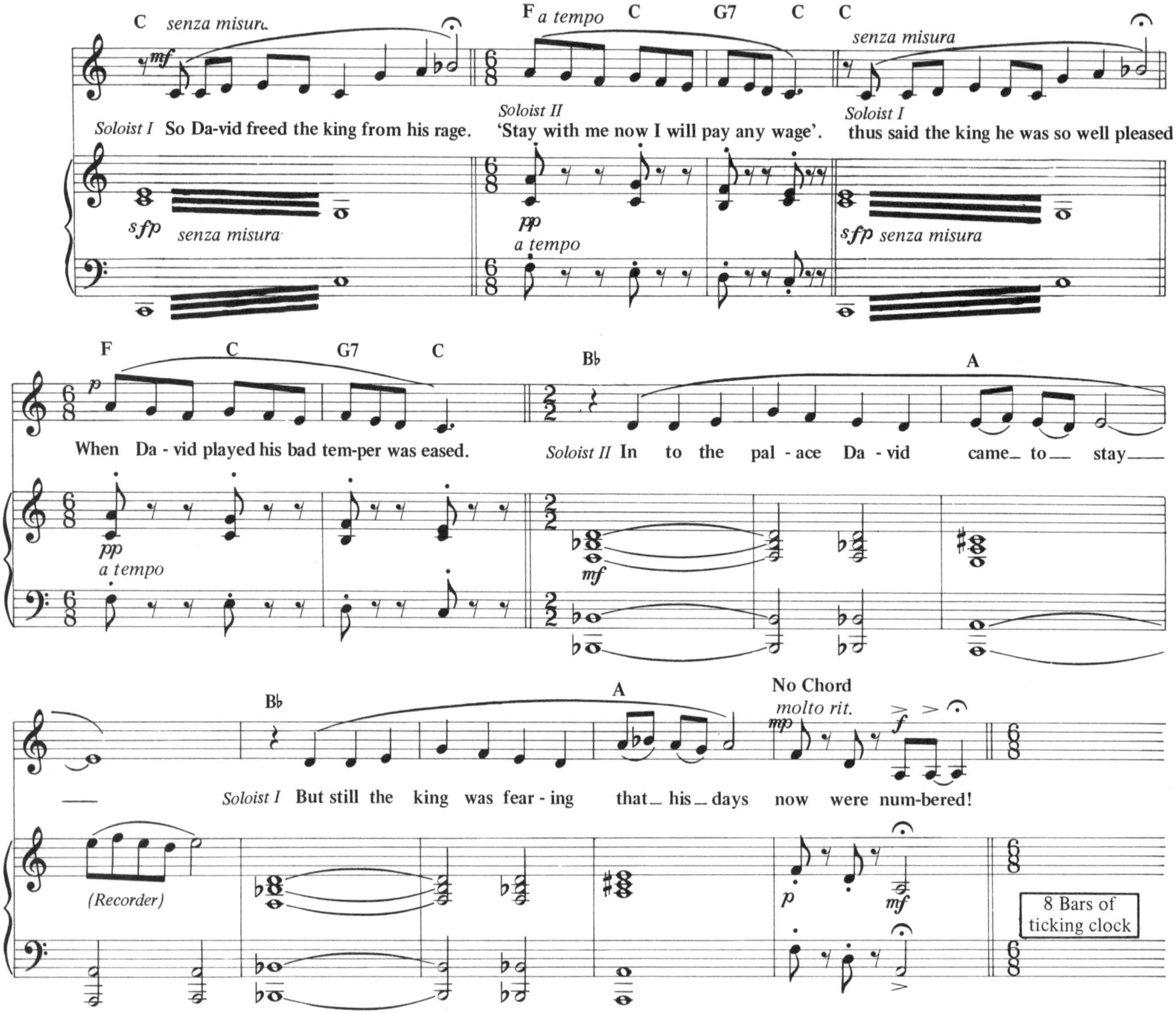

C *senza misura* — F *a tempo* C G7 C — C *senza misura*

Soloist I So Da-vid freed the king from his rage. *Soloist II* 'Stay with me now I will pay any wage'. *Soloist I* thus said the king he was so well pleased.

sfp senza misura — *pp a tempo* — *sfp senza misura*

F C G7 C — B♭ — A

When Da - vid played his bad tem-per was eased. *Soloist II* In to the pal - ace Da - vid came — to — stay —

pp a tempo — *mf*

B♭ — A — No Chord *molto rit.*

Soloist I But still the king was fear - ing that — his — days now were num-bered!

(Recorder) — *p* — *mf*

8 Bars of ticking clock

9. Song Of The Kings (Part 2)

(2 Soloists and Chorus)

mp
King Saul was ag - ing
f
mf
8va
Bb
Ab
Eb
Bb
Bb
Ab
mf
Soloist I Out in the fields his fine ar - mies were scared
Soloist II
One called Go - li - ath his
mp
8va
Eb
Bb
Ebm
E
F
Bb
Ebm
E
sol - diers had dared. So Da - vid went out there so bold so a - lone, and killed the great gi - ant with sling and a
Soloist I
Soloist II
mp
F
ff
stone. CHORUS Sling and a stone.
8va
ff
CHORUS King Saul was scream - ing!
f
8va

mp
King Saul was schem - ing.
mf
8va
C Bb F C C Bb F C
mf
Soloist I As the years passed he got jeal - ous you see. Soloist II Da - vid had grown much more fa-mous than he.
Soloist I
So
mp
C Fm Gb G C Fm Gb G
time af - ter time a new plan he'd de - vise,
Soloist II
to kill off this up-start, to bring his de - mise,
mp
ff
CHORUS Bring his de - mise!
f
ff
8va
ff
King Saul was flam - ing.
f
8va

mp
King Saul was wan - ing.
mf
8va
D C G D D C G D D Gm
mf
Soloist I All of his plans seemed to go quite a - stray.
Soloist II
Da - vid was win-ning more bat-tles each day,
Soloist I
and when Da - vid spared him his
mp
Ab A D Gm Ab A
molto rit.
ff
life with a grin, he gave up the ti - tle and Da - vid was king
Soloist II
CHORUS Da - vid was
mp
molto rit.
a tempo
king!
a tempo
f
8va
ff
Da - vid was king!
ff
fff
8va

10. So The Bible Says

(Chorus)

11. He Could Tell

(Soloist — boy preferably — and Chorus)

f
Bb7
CHORUS He could tell,
He could tell,
mf
Soloist 1. In the years – to – come, – there'd be no
2. they would have – to – pay, – for they must
mf
8va
Eb7
Bb7
He could tell,
He could tell,
– more – fun, – for the Jews – un – true, – God would turn – the – screw, –
– o - bey, – that their wars – must cease. – that there must – be – peace. –
8va
F
Eb
Bb7
mp
mf
f
He – could – tell us some more, – tell us some more, – tell us some more, –
He could tell.
mp
mf
f
8va
1
2
ff
ff
Gb
f
Ebm
tell us some more. He could tell tell us some more. – I-sai-ah! I-sai-ah! I - sai - - -
f
I - sai - ah! I - sai - ah! I - sai - - -
ff
8va
8va

Gb
(tacet)
- - - ah!
I-sai-ah!
I-sai-ah! I-sai
- - - ah! I-sai-ah! I-sai-ah! I-sai
Db
No Chord
(hand claps)
Bb7
- ah!
I-sai-ah!
(foot stamps)
- ah!
I-sai-ah!
ff
mf
8va
f
Bb7
CHORUS He could tell,
mf
Soloist 3. They must trust
4. There would be
mf
8va
Eb7
To Coda
He could tell,
He could tell,
in God,
a man.
he would spare no rod.
it was in the plan.
they would have
he'd bring peace
8va

Bb7
He could tell,
F
Eb
He could
to cope,
that they must have hope.
He could
Bb7
mp
tell us some more,
mf
tell us some more,
f
tell us some more,
tell.
8va
ff
D.%. al Coda
tell us some more, he could tell,
CODA
No Chord
molto rit.
He could tell.
Regular but slower speed than before
Em - man - u - el
you'd see.
and his name would be
Em - man - u - el
Em - man - u - el
Segue

12. Emmanuel (Part 1)

(Chorus)

13. Ever Bowing, Ever Scraping

(The Choir divided into two groups I & II)

14. Emmanuel (Part 2)
(Chorus)
♩= 126
Dm Am Dm Dm
(Recorders)
mf
CHORUS 1. Slaves of King Her-od, we're the slaves of king Her-od, Oh Re-deem - - er!
2. Spare us from ev - il, from the man-y kinds of ev-il, Oh Re-deem - - er!
C
Save us from Her - od, come and save us from Her-od Oh Re-
Though we are sin - ners, we are sor-ry we are sin-ners, Oh Re-
Dm
deem - - er!
deem - - er!
F C B♭ F B♭ F C F C
mp
Come, oh come, from your kingdom up there, from your kingdom up there a - bove. Come oh come, to your
B♭ F B♭ F C F
peo-ple on earth, to your peo-ple on earth bring love.
f
Em - man - u - el! Em -
B♭ F C F
- man - u - el! Em - man - u - el!
1 F
2 F
- el!
8va

PART II 15. In A Town Called Nazareth

(Chorus)

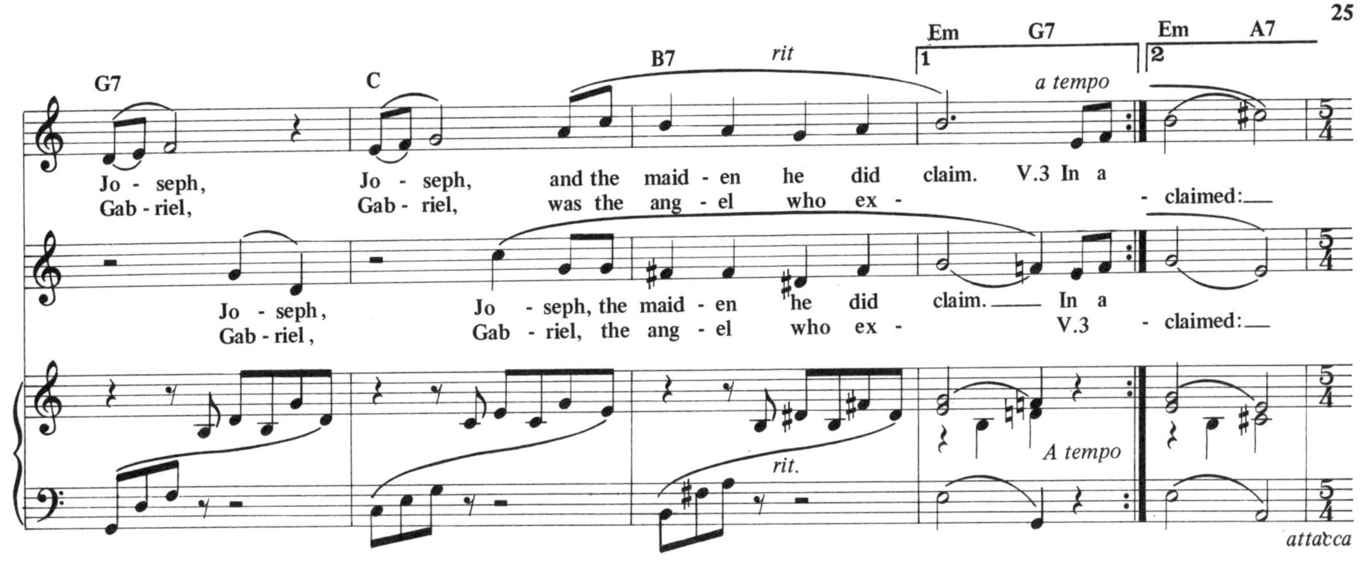

16. Hail Mary

(Soloist and Chorus)

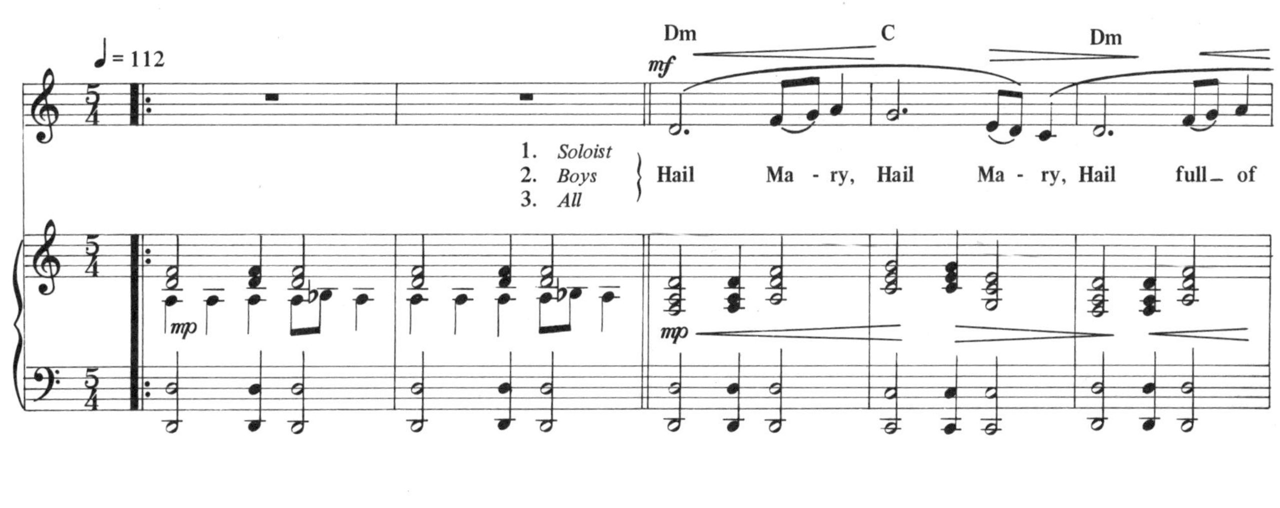

Am
mf
G
F
G
Soloist
V.1. The Lord is wi-th thee, and he will al-ways be Through all e-ter-ni-ty.
V.2. You are to bear a son, share him with ev'ry-one On you the spi-rit will come.
mp
Am
G
F
E
1
You must not be a-fraid, his will must be o-beyed, your part must now be played.
Son of the most high, Lord of the sea and sky, his king-dom never will
mp
2
E
die.
D.C. al Coda
CODA
E
Am
G
rit.
F
Em
CHORUS Hail Ma-ry full of
rit.
A a tempo
grace A-men
a tempo

17. The Son of God (A Magnificat)

(Girl Soloist and Chorus)

18. How Can It Be?

(Joseph and Chorus)

Em+5 Em B Em B Em Em+7
think that he knew what our fu-ture held in store. An-gel I say. can you cre-dit it in
fear it would seem just take Ma-ry as my kin. Then, God knows why. by the po-wer of the
Em7 Em6 Em+5 Em E♭
this age and day, has our mar-riage got to start in this way. She's sim-ply clutching at a straw, I'm
spi-rit on high, Ma-ry bears a son called Je-sus who'll die and yet he'll save the world from sin strange
D D G F
sure. thing. CHORUS How can it be? How can it hap-pen to be? It could
Em B Em B G F
happen to any man you see. How can it be? How can it hap-pen to be? It could
Em B rit. E rit. E dim7 E
hap-pen to a-ny man you see. Joseph Why me?

19. Order From Rome

(Chorus in unison)

20. So The Bible Says

(Chorus)

21. Bethlehem Is A Long Way

(Chorus)

C F C F C G7 C
I
La la la — la la la la la la la la la — la la la la la — la la
II
Beth - le - hem — is a long way, a long way, far too far — for us. Get there quick - ly don't
F C F C G7 C F B♭ F B♭ F
la la la la la la la la la la la — la la la la la la
de - lay, don't de - lay for fear of your life ! Keep to - geth - er and don't stay, no don't stay,
C7 F B♭ F B♭ F C7 F C7 F
1 2
la la la — la la la la la — la la la la la la la la la la la la la la la
far a - way from us. God be with us all we pray, yes we pray be with us to-day. with us to - day.
CODA
C F C C F C C F C C F C
La la la — la la la la la la la — la la la la la la la — la la la la la la la — la la la la.
diminuendo
(stop bongos)
(stop Shakers)

22. Shelter Me Friend

(Chorus)

poco rit.
A7
Dm
mp
a tempo
with the ut - most care he led her.
in a crib of hay he laid him.
2. To a corn - er of the cav - ern,
4. Then he knelt there just be - side her,
poco rit.
a tempo
C
C
Dm
C
on a sto - ny floor,
they be - gan to pray,
ve - ry slow - ly, ve - ry gent - ly,
both to - ge - ther, close to - ge - ther,
F
D
mf
on a bed of straw he laid her.
hop - ing that they may be wor - thy.
Lit a lamp there, and the light's flare
Can the glo - ry, of this sto - ry,
Gm
Dm
1 A7
helped to re - as - sure;
as the pro - phets say,
so they wait - ed, un - til they could
come to be true,
Dm
2 A7
Dm
rit.
keep a - wake no more
is he the one to save the world one day?
rit.
pp

24(a). Shepherd, Lonely Shepherd

(Recorders)

24(b). Shepherds, Lonely Shepherds

(2 Soloists and Chorus)

A♭ G No chord C G
they must watch their sheep; watch their sheep.
stars are shin - ing still; shin - ing still.
3
mp
8ve
C C G 1 C 2 C C G7
mf
CHORUS "Shep - herds, lone - ly
C C G C F
shep - herds, do not be a - fraid! Go now to the
C G7 C B♭
ci - ty, there in a man - ger laid you'll find a child born, all

A♭ C G7 C B♭ A♭
wrapped in swad - dling clothes. He is the Sav - iour ar - riv - ing as he
G No Chord C G7 C G7
chose, as he chose. Ah Ah.
mp
8ve
C C G7 C C G
mf
Soloists I+II Shep - herds, lone - ly shep - herds; shep - herds up - on the
C F C G7
hill; watch - ing as the an - gels sing now the air they

C
recorders or Semi-Chorus
No Chord
f
Ah.
S.
A.
T.
B.
fill. "To God in Heaven be glo - ry ev - er more, and to his
piano optional
f
Ah.
Then we see them no more
Soloists I+II
friends peace on earth he will re - store."
CHORUS
Ah,
mf
Ah.
Ah,
mp
Ah
Ah.
rit
mp

25. Surely Angels Must Know

(Chorus)

A7
Dm
go.
too.
V.2. Soon in - to the ci - ty came the shep - herds
V.4. Peer - ing in the man - ger where the babe is
C
Dm
C
search - ing:
sleep - ing:
Not an ea - sy task to find there the
see - ing him they kneel and join in the
F
D
cave.
prayer.
Sure - ly an - gels must
Sure - ly an - gels must
Gm
Dm
A7
know.
know.
help us find the man - ger and the ba - by
here we have the Sav - iour bring - ing peace to
1 Dm
2 Dm
boy.
all.
rit.

26. Far Away From Eastern Lands

(Chorus)

27(a). Holy Child

(Chorus)

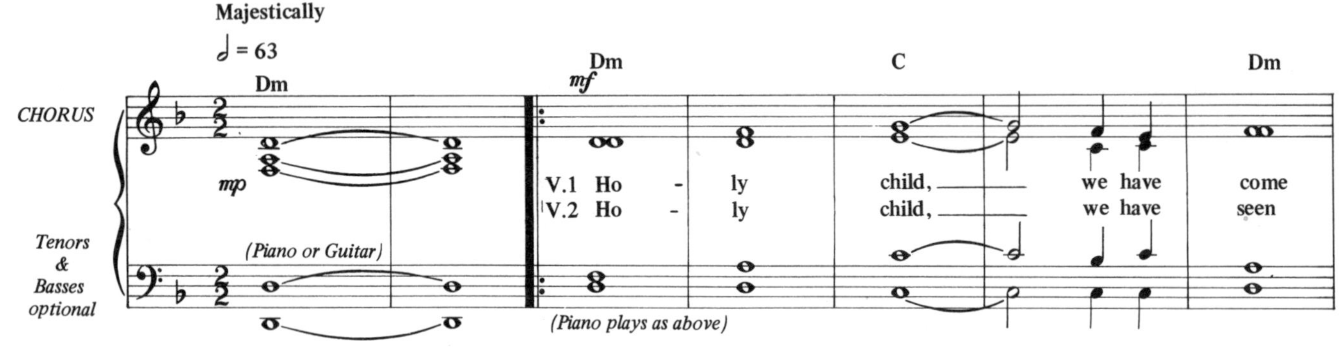

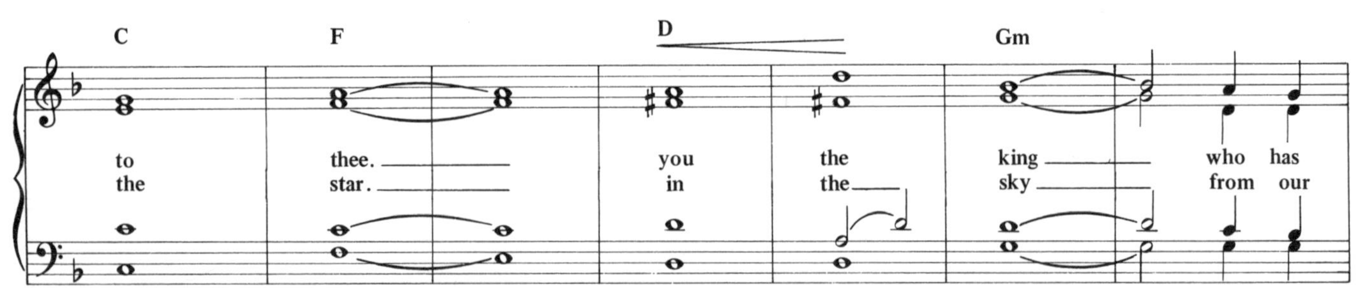

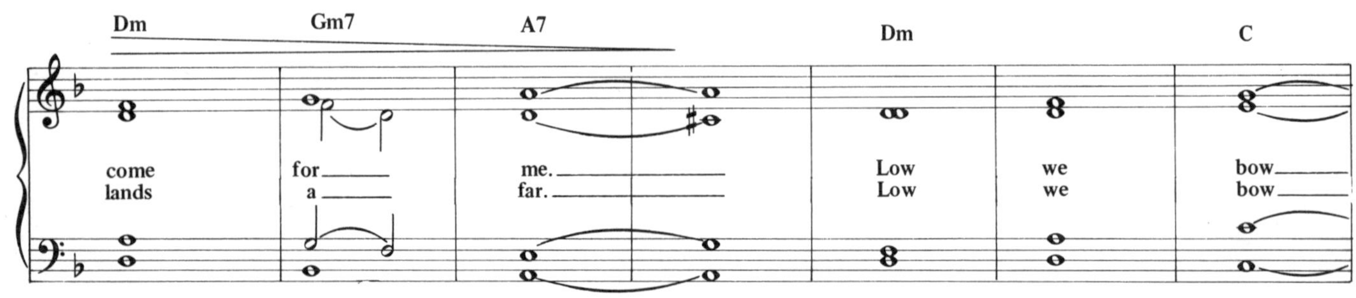

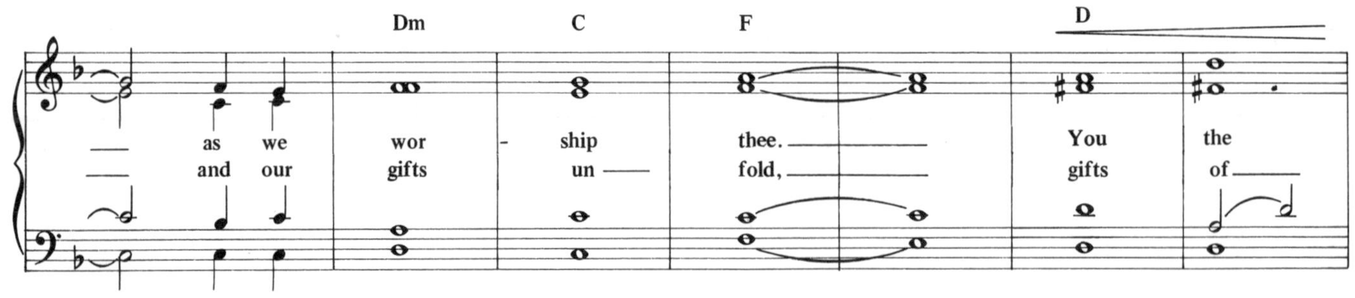

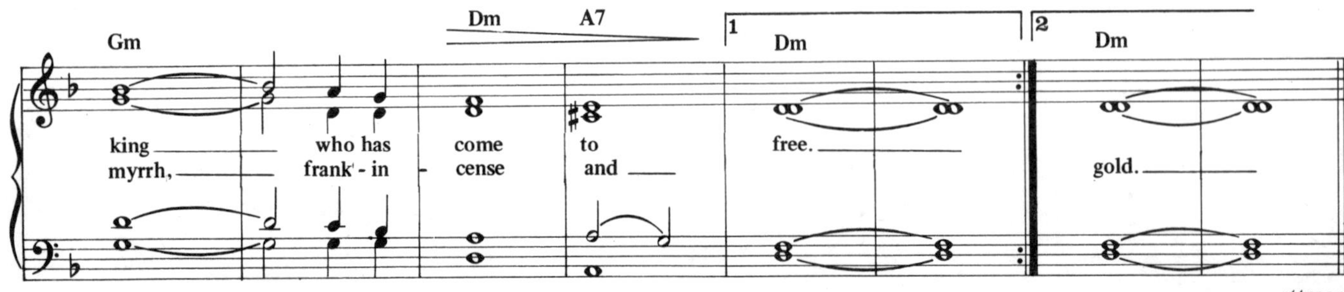

27(b). Holy Child/In The Darkness

(Chorus divides into two)

Dm
C
Dm
C
Low we bow, as we wor - - ship
To a corn-er of the cav-ern, on a sto-ny floor, ve-ry slow-ly, ve-ry gent-ly,
F
D
Gm
thee. You the King
on a bed of straw he laid her. Lit a lamp there, and the light's flare helped to re-as-
Dm
A7
Dm
who has come to free.
-sure; so they wait-ed un-til they could keep a-wake no more.

27(c). Holy Child/In The Darkness/ Surely Angels Must Know

(Chorus divides into three)

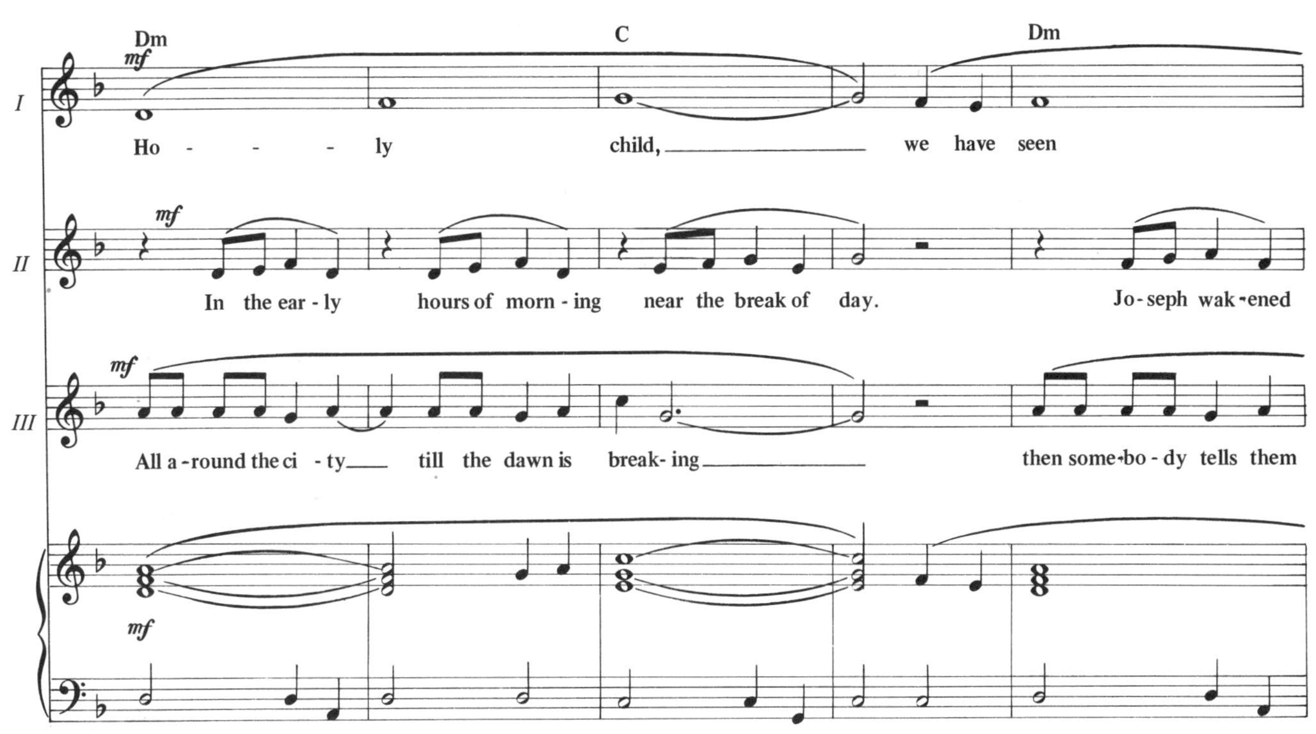

C F D

the star, in the

from his dream - ing, looked a - cross the way to Ma - ry, and he saw their lit - tle boy there

'Down there the cave;' Sure - ly an - gels must

Gm
Dm
A7
sky from our lands a far
in her arms he lay. Took him gent - ly, held him up and in a crib of
know; here's the ba - by Je - sus, Ma - ry, Jo - seph too.
Dm
mf
C
Low we bow, and our
hay he laid him. Then he knelt there just be - side her, they be - gan to pray;
Peer - ing in the mang - er where the babe is sleep - ing,
Dm
C
F
D
gifts un fold. Gifts
both to - ge - ther, close to - ge - ther, hop - ing that they may be worth - y. Can the glo - ry
see - ing him they kneel and join in the prayer. Sure - ly

Gm Dm A7

of myrrh, ______, fran - kin - cense and

of this stor - y, as the proph-ets say, come to be true, is he the one to

an - gels must know ______, here we have the Sav - iour ______ bring-ing peace to

Dm B♭ *mf* C D

gold. ______ The Ho - ly ______ child. ______

mf

save the world one day? The Ho - ly ______ child. ______

f

all. ______ The ______

mf

f

f

f

C D C D E

f

______ The Ho - ly, ______ Ho - ly Child. ______

f

______ The Ho - - ly, ______ Ho - ly Child. ______

Ho - ly, Ho - ly, Ho - ly ______ Child. ______

f

molto rit.

fff

28. Song Of The Kings (Part 3)

(2 Soloists and Chorus)

E
F
ff
out look was
grim !
CHORUS Out - look was
grim !
VERSE 2
ff
CHORUS He - rod was sneer - ing !
ff
f
mp
He - rod was fear - ing.
mf
mf
C
B♭
F
C
C
B♭
Soloist I
He did - n't know the wise men had a dream
Soloist II
tell - ing them "Has - ten a -
mp

F C C Fm G♭ G C Fm
way from the scene!" They could-n't tell He-rod, that wick-ed old man! a-void-ing Je-ru-sa-lem
Soloist I
Soloist II
mp
G♭ G
was the best plan.
CHORUS Was the best plan!
Trem.
VERSE 3
ff
CHORUS He-rod was scream-ing!
f

mp
He - rod was schem - ing.
mf
D C G D D C G D
mf
Soloist I
As the wise men had - n't turned up to tell,
Soloist II
he'd pun - ish Beth - le - hem, make their life hell!
Soloist I
So
mp
D Gm Ab A D Gm Ab
all the boy ba - bies who were un - der two,
Soloist II
he put them to death that would show them who's
mp
molto rit.
A
ff
who!
CHORUS
show them who's who!
molto rit.
ff

29. Recit: Now the Baby Boys Are Slaughtered

(2 Soloists)

30. How Can It Be?

(Joseph and Chorus)

B
Em
B
mf
Em
a - ny man, why me? Last night in my dreams,
mf
Em+7
Em7
Em6
Em+5
came a mess-en-ger to warn me it seems I can't hope to know what all of this means,
poco cresc.
Em
B
Em
B
Em
f
I just lis - ten in dis - may "Go now" said he,
f
Em+7
Em7
Em6
Em+5
"With your wife and child from here you must flee, in - to Eg - ypt, and you'll wait there for me."
Em
E♭
D
poco rit.
So God be with us on our way, I pray.
poco rit

a tempo
mf
G
F
CHORUS Now can't you see how all this hap-pened to
a tempo
mf
Em
B
Em
be. it could have hap-pened to a-ny man you see.
B
G
F
But you were the man, you were the right kind of
Em
B
man you were part of God's spec-ial plan, you see?
E
Edim7
E
Joseph I see.

31. Holy Boy

(Mary Joseph and Chorus)

Ebsus
meek and low - ly, such a Ho - ly
man - ger low - ly, for the Ho - ly
par - ents low - ly, for the Ho - ly
shep - herds low - ly, see the Ho - ly
bow so low - ly, to the Ho - ly
Bb Ab Bb
No Chord
Bb
mf
Boy.
Boy. CHORUS He came to save the world. He came to
Boy.
Boy.
Boy.
mf
8va
save the hu - man race, and when we leave this
world we go to meet him face to face.
1-4
5
He came to

CHORUS divides into 2
B♭
I
save the world, he came to save the hu - man race, and when we
II
Ho - ly, yes he's the boy that's ho - ly. Ho - ly, yes he's the boy that's ho - ly.
leave this world we go to meet him face to face. He came to
Ho - ly, yes he's the boy that's ho - ly. Ho - ly, yes he's the boy that's ho - ly.
CHORUS divides into 3
B♭
I
save the world, he came to save the hu - man race, and when we
II
Ho - ly, yes he's the boy that's ho - ly. Ho - ly, yes he's the boy that's ho - ly.
III
Meek and low - ly, such a ho - ly,

leave this world we go to meet him face to face. Ho-ly Boy
Ho-ly, yes he's the boy that's ho-ly. Ho-ly, yes he's the boy, that Ho-ly Boy
meek and low-ly, such a Ho-ly Boy
C
Bb
C
Bb
ff
Ho-ly Boy, Ho-ly Boy,
(in octaves)
C
Bb
C
fff
Ho-ly Boy!

Printed in Great Britain by Hobbs the Printers of Southampton